NOW THAT I BELIEVE

I know the Lord will
bring you much joy &
speak to you through His
word.

6-17-86

Carol

NOW THAT
I BELIEVE

by

ROBERT A.   COOK
President, The Kings College

MOODY PRESS

CHICAGO

97 98 99 100 101 102 Printing/LC/Year 88 87 86 85 84 83

Printed in the United States of America

INTRODUCTION

Anything from the pen of Dr. Robert Cook is not only very good reading but it is important. "NOW THAT I BELIEVE," written by this young man for young people, has grown out of his own experience of salvation. It is Biblical, dynamic, and soul-stirring.

"NOW THAT I BELIEVE" is not optional. It is a MUST for every young man and young woman who wants to make progress and be victorious in the Christian Life. We recommend this volume as being most profitable for widespread distribution especially among Christian young people.

DR. TORREY M. JOHNSON

*   *   *   *   *

Medical and scientific resources are constantly being employed and increased to combat the rather high mortality rate among children in their first year of life, due to the diseases peculiar to that period. It is not what it was years ago, but it is still

5

high, according to the Public Health Service, National Office, statistics for 1963.

It seems to me that the spiritual mortality rate among "babes in Christ" is high, if we are to judge by the growth of our evangelical churches, and the extension of our home and foreign missionary effort. The reasons for it, and the opinions expressed about it may be legion, but I believe that the use of this book by pastors and Christian workers dealing with young Christians will result in a diminishing number of confused, frustrated, backsliding, emaciated beginners in the Christian life, and an increase in spiritual stalwarts. To this end, I recommend the extensive use of this book.

CEDRIC SEARS

THIS BOOK . . .

. . . presupposes the new birth. Of course it is impossible to live the Christian life until one has started that existence—been born again. Remind yourself right now that the supreme value in this world is to be right with God through faith in Jesus Christ. If there is any doubt whatever about that relationship, get down on your knees, confess your sins, and receive the Lord Jesus, by faith, into your life.

"But as many as received him, to them gave he power to become the sons of God, even to them that believe on his name" (John 1:12). For immediate, thoughtful consideration of the Scripture used in this book, and only where the small reference numeral is used, we refer you to the closing portion of each chapter.

CONTENTS

I walk in a daze and yet am conscious. I know myself to be a citizen of another world, but live familiarly in this one. I sense a change in my desires, convictions, beliefs, but am still the same personality. I love my friends and long for their salvation but am strangely out of step with their pagan way of life. I weep where once I laughed, and laugh where once I wept. I am tender where once I was ruthless, yet unyielding where once I gave way to pressures and temptations. I am a new person, yet the same person. . . . What happened to me?

1

WHAT HAPPENED TO ME?

A MIRACLE

You, my friend, are a direct proof of the statement that the age of miracles is not past. For you, yourself, are a miracle. God's description of a Christian indicates that fact most clearly: "Therefore if any man be in Christ, he is a new creature [creation]: old things are passed away; behold, all things are become new" (II Cor. 5:17).

Our Lord Jesus made this truth His basic approach to one of the most learned men in His day—Nicodemus.[1]

"Nicodemus," He said, "you must be born again. If not, you'll never see the kingdom of God."

Nicodemus raised an immediate objection.

"How can these things be?" Perplexity, the result of an unsaved heart trying to analyze salvation, was in his voice.

Our Lord answered patiently, tenderly. "Nicodemus," He said, "marvel not that I said unto thee, Ye must be born again. You can't explain it — true. But you can't explain a lot of other things, either. Take the wind, for instance. Can you tell where it came from, and where it is going? No. You can feel it, hear it whispering through the leaves, but you can't explain it. Neither can you explain salvation.

"Here's the difficulty," He continued. "You were born once, with an earthly nature. You're a sinner, Nicodemus, and you have a sinful nature. That which is born of the flesh is flesh . . . and nothing more! How do you ever expect to get past the judgment of a holy God with nothing but sinful flesh? You have to have another birth, Nicodemus, a birth from above. Let's call it a birth of the Spirit, because He's the One who is active in it. When *that* occurs, you'll have a new, holy nature, for that which is born of the Spirit is spirit."

Essentially, salvation is the miracle of receiving life. There is nothing so hopelessly still as a corpse. No scientist has yet been able to breathe life into a dead body. Just as hopeless is the sinner without Christ. He is "dead in trespasses and sins."[2] Nor has he any prospect of doing better, for "they that are in the flesh cannot please God" (Rom. 8:8).

Our Lord Jesus emphasized this truth when He said: "It is the Spirit that quickeneth; the flesh profiteth nothing: the words that I speak unto you, they are spirit, and they are life" (John 6:63). And "he that heareth my word, and believeth on him that sent me, hath everlasting life, and shall not come into condemnation [judgment], but is passed from death unto life" (John 5:24).

Yes, a miracle happened to you when you were saved. The Lord Jesus touched your life with His nail-scarred hand and gave you new life, with a new nature—*His* life, and *His* nature!

YOU MET A WONDERFUL PERSON

Salvation is not something you do, but something Christ does when you receive Him. "But as many as received him, to them gave he power to become the sons of God, even to them that believe on his name" (John 1:12). Personal testimonies in the Gospels and the Acts highlight this fact.

Andrew, talking to Simon Peter: "We have found the Messias, which is, being interpreted, the Christ. And he brought him to Jesus" (John 1:41).

Philip, to Nathanael: "We have found him, of whom Moses in the law, and the prophets, did write, Jesus of Nazareth, the son of Joseph" (John 1:45).

The woman of Samaria: "Come, see a man, which told me all things that ever I did: is not this the Christ?" (John 4:29).

Paul, before Agrippa: "At midday, O king, I saw . . . a light, and I heard a voice . . . and I said, Who art thou, Lord? And he said, I am Jesus whom thou persecutest. But rise, and stand upon thy feet: for I have appeared unto thee for this purpose, to make thee a minister and a witness both of these things which thou hast seen, and of those things in the which I will appear unto thee."[3]

It is easy to see why this personal emphasis must be. *Only a person could reveal God to me:* "He that came down from heaven . . .[4] The only begotten Son, which is in the bosom of the Father, he hath declared him."[5] *Only a person could meet my personal need and heal sin's deadly sting:* "And as Moses lifted up the serpent in the wilderness, even so must the Son of man be lifted up: that whosoever believeth in him should not perish, but have eternal life"

(John 3:14, 15). *Only a person*—a divine Person—*could bestow everlasting life:* "For God so loved the world, that he gave his only begotten Son, that whosoever believeth in him should not perish, but have everlasting life" (John 3:16). And *it takes a person to satisfy and keep me:* "Ye are complete in him [6] . . . for all things are yours; whether Paul, or Apollos, or Cephas, or the world, or life, or death, or things present, or things to come; all are yours; and ye are Christ's; and Christ is God's" (I Cor. 3:21-23). When I approach God, I am accepted "in the Beloved"[7]—*a Person*—and my daily goal is to "be found *in him,* not having mine own righteousness, which is of the law, but that which is through the faith of Christ, the righteousness which is of God by faith" (Phil. 3:9).

Salvation is not something—it's Somebody! When you were saved, you met a Person, you opened your life to Him, and you are now living under His control. Paul said: "I know *whom* I have believed, and am persuaded that *he* is able to keep that which I have committed unto *him* against that day."[8]

YOU BECAME PART OF AN
ETERNAL TRANSACTION

"For what saith the scripture? Abraham believed God, and it was counted unto him for righteousness. Now to him that worketh is the reward not reckoned of grace, but of debt. But to him that worketh not, but believeth on him that justifieth the ungodly, *his faith is counted for righteousness*" (Rom 4:3-5).

Let us get the picture straight. What does God demand? Righteousness.

What can I offer? Only sin and more sin.[9]

Can I ever hope to do better under my own power? No, because I am condemned already without Christ.[10]

How may I obtain the righteousness that God demands? Simply by receiving it by faith.[11]

When I receive Christ, does that alter my standing before God? Certainly it does. God takes the righteousness of Christ and puts it to my account. Because Jesus died for me, God can both "be just, and the justifier of him which believeth in Jesus" (Rom. 3:26).

Someone says, "I still don't understand it."

Look then at this verse: "God was in Christ, reconciling the world unto himself, not imputing their trespasses unto them . . . for he hath made him [Christ] to be sin for us, [He] who knew no sin; that we might be made the righteousness of God in him."[12] Who was sinned against? God.

Who alone could settle the score of sin? God.

Who was it, suffering on the cross for sin? God.

Has the debt been paid? Yes, because "the Lord hath laid on him the iniquity of us all,"[13] and He "himself bare our sins in his own body on the tree, that we, being dead to sins, should live unto righteousness: by whose stripes ye were healed" (I Peter 2:24).

If *God* is the one sinned against and *God* has paid the debt and settled the score, does *God* have a right to give to me, freely, His righteousness? Yes, hallelujah! it is free: "even the righteousness of God which is by faith of Jesus Christ unto and upon all them that believe . . . being justified freely by his grace through the redemption that is in Christ Jesus" (Rom. 3:22, 24).

Here, then, is the transaction that takes place at conversion: God forgives my sin,[14] imputes and imparts His righteousness, [15] makes me forever His child,[16] and gives me an inheritance with Christ.[17] *He* does it, mind you, not I. No wonder we shout, Hallelujah, what a Saviour!

This is what happened to you. You experienced a miracle: you met a Person, and you became part of an eternal transaction.

Every part of this truth is initiated by, and dependent upon, Almighty God. If He started it, He certainly will finish it. All of which brings us to a discussion of the unspoken fear of every new convert: What if my Christian joy should not last? Turn to chapter 2, and see what God's Word says on the subject.

COORDINATE SCRIPTURE FOR
CHAPTER 1

1. There was a man of the Pharisees, named Nicodemus, a ruler of the Jews: the same came to Jesus by night, and said unto him, Rabbi, we know that thou art a teacher come from God: for no man can do these miracles that thou doest, except God be with him.

Jesus answered and said unto him, Verily, verily, I say unto thee, Except a man be born again, he cannot see the kingdom of God.

Nicodemus saith unto him, How can a man be born when he is old? can he enter the second time into his mother's womb, and be born?

Jesus answered, Verily, verily, I say unto thee, Except a man be born of water and of the Spirit, he cannot enter into the kingdom of God.

That which is born of the flesh is flesh; and that which is born of the Spirit is spirit. Marvel not that I said unto thee, Ye must be born again. The wind bloweth where it listeth, and thou hearest the sound thereof, but canst not tell whence it cometh, and whither it goeth: so is every one that is born of the Spirit.

Nicodemus answered and said unto him, How can these things be?

Jesus answered and said unto him, Art thou a master of Israel, and knowest not these things? Verily, verily, I say unto thee, We speak that we do know, and testify that we have seen; and ye receive not our witness.

If I have told you earthly things, and ye believe not, how shall ye believe, if I tell you of heavenly things?

And no man hath ascended up to heaven, but he that came down from heaven, even the Son of man which is in heaven.

And as Moses lifted up the serpent in the wilderness, even so must the Son of man be lifted up:

That whosoever believeth in him should not perish, but have eternal life. For God so loved the world, that he gave his only begotten Son, that whosoever believeth in him should not perish, but have everlasting life.—John 3:1-16.

2.   And you hath he quickened, who were dead in trespasses and sins.—Ephesians 2:1.

3.   Whereupon as I went to Damascus with authority and commission from the chief priests,

At midday, O king, I saw in the way a light from heaven, above the brightness of the sun, shining round about me and them which journeyed with me.

And when we were all fallen to the earth, I heard a voice speaking unto me, and saying in the Hebrew tongue, Saul, Saul, why persecutest thou me? it is hard for thee to kick against the pricks.

And I said, Who art thou, Lord? And he said, I am Jesus whom thou persecutest.

But rise, and stand upon thy feet: for I have appeared unto thee for this purpose, to make thee a minister and a witness both of these things which thou hast seen, and of those things in the which I will appear unto thee;

Delivering thee from the people, and from the Gentiles, unto whom now I send thee,

To open their eyes, and to turn them from darkness to light, and from the power of Satan unto God, that they may receive forgiveness of sins, and inheritance among them which are sanctified by faith that is in me.

Whereupon, O king Agrippa, I was not disobedient unto the heavenly vision:

But showed first unto them of Damascus, and at Jerusalem, and throughout all the coasts of Judea, and then to the Gentiles, that they should repent and turn to God, and do works meet for repentance.— Acts 26:12-20.

4. And no man hath ascended up to heaven, but he that came down from heaven, even the Son of man which is in heaven.— John 3:13.

5. No man hath seen God at any time: the only begotten Son, which is in the bosom of the Father, he hath declared him.— John 1:18.

6. And ye are complete in him, which is the head of all principality and power.— Colossians 2:10.

7. To the praise of the glory of his grace, wherein he hath made us accepted in the beloved.— Ephesians 1:6.

8. For the which cause I also suffer these things: nevertheless I am not ashamed: for I know whom I have believed, and am persuaded that he is able to keep that which I have committed unto him against that day.— II Timothy 1:12.

9. As it is written, There is none righteous, no, not one:

There is none that understandeth, there is none that seeketh after God.

They are all gone out of the way, they are together become unprofitable; there is none that doeth good, no, not one.

Their throat *is* an open sepulchre; with their tongues they have used deceit; the poison of asps *is* under their lips:

Whose mouth *is* full of cursing and bitterness:
Their feet *are* swift to shed blood:
Destruction and misery *are* in their ways:
And the way of peace have they not known:
There is no fear of God before their eyes:

Now we know, that what things soever the law saith, it saith to them who are under the law; that every mouth may be stopped, and all the world may become guilty before God.

Therefore by the deeds of the law there shall no flesh be justified in his sight: for by the law *is* the knowledge of sin.— Romans 3:10-20

10.   He that believeth on him is not condemned; but he that believeth not is condemned already, because he hath not believed in the name of the only begotten Son of God.— John 3:18.

11.   Even the righteousness of God, *which is* by faith of Jesus Christ, unto all and upon all them that believe: for there is no difference.— Romans 3:22.

12.   To wit, that God was in Christ, reconciling the world unto himself, not imputing their trespasses unto them; and hath committed unto us the word of reconciliation.

Now then we are ambassadors for Christ, as though God did beseech *you* by us: we pray *you* in Christ's stead, be ye reconciled to God.

For he hath made him *to be* sin for us, who knew no sin; that we might be made the righteousness of God in him.— II Corinthians 5:19-21.

13.   All we, like sheep, have gone astray; we have turned every one to his own way; and the LORD hath laid on him the iniquity of us all.—Isaiah 53:6.

14.   And you, being dead in your sins and the uncircumcision of your flesh, hath he quickened together with him, having forgiven you all trespasses.— Colossians 2:13.

15.   Even the righteousness of God which is by faith of Jesus Christ unto all and upon all of them that believe: for there is no difference.— Romans 3:22.

16.   But as many as received him, to them gave he power to become the sons of God, even to them that believe on his name.— John 1:12.

17.   The Spirit itself beareth witness with our spirit, that we are the children of God:
And if children, then heirs; heirs of God, and joint-heirs with Christ; if so be that we suffer with him, that we may be also glorified together.—Romans 8:16, 17.

For the first time in my life, I know joy. Happiness, I have had . . . fleeting enjoyment, based on things, and circumstances, and people. I have learned by experience that the pleasures of sin "are but for a season." And I have known the staleness of surfeit, the acrid taste of disappointment, the bitterness of regret, the utterly unsatisfying nature of all things earthy.

Now, I have joy — the pure delight of a soul that is right with God. What if . . . what if something should destroy that relation? What if I fail? What if the joy does not last?

2

HOW LONG WILL THIS NEW-FOUND JOY LAST?

Your joy is not an end in itself, but a result. It comes from the fact that you are in a right relationship to God through faith in Christ.

Even this relationship is not an end in itself. It stems in turn from the eternal purposes of God Almighty. "Known unto God are all his works from the beginning of the world" (Acts 15:18). Paul speaks of Christians as those who are "called according to his purpose."[1] Christians were chosen in Christ "before the foundation of the world."[2]

You thought your Christian life started when you knelt at Calvary, and so it did. But at the same time, you stepped into the mighty current of the purpose of God, and all that you are today depends upon your relation to that eternal plan.

It is necessary that you see this truth clearly. Humanly, we tend to think of ourselves as being quite important. Prove this by asking yourself whose picture you look for *first* in any group photo! God's point of view is entirely different. When we stand at the cross and look at life with Him, we are not nearly so important as we thought. Rather, His will . . . His plan . . . His purpose become the main issues of our lives.

"Very well," you say. "I know that my joy comes *from* God. But that is not my trouble. Now, what if I should lose it? Then what?"

Before you worry further, turn to the Word. "According to the eternal purpose which he purposed in Christ Jesus our Lord" (Eph. 3:11).

What kind of purpose is it, of which you are a part?

An *eternal* purpose.

How long is an eternal purpose?

Forever and ever.

Is that long enough to see me through this life and get me to heaven? If it is, then what am I worrying about?

This is the sense of that blessed promise in Philippians: "Being confident of this very thing, that he which hath begun a good work in you will perform it until the day of Jesus Christ" (Phil. 1:6).

If God planned it, initiated it, saw it to fruition in my soul, tied His almightiness and His heavenly reputation to it, then certainly I ought to trust Him with the working out of His eternal purpose.

Many a failure in the Christian life originates right here. People often come to me and say, "I'm through . . . I've failed . . . I can't keep up the Christian life." Frequently I'll answer them, "Well, praise God."

Shocked they will ask, "What is there to praise God about?"

Simply, the answer is this: Thank God you've discovered that you cannot produce nor can you maintain the Christian life. God must do it, or it simply isn't done! More about this later.

How long will my joy last? As long as God is God and His Word is truth . . . as long as the eternal purpose of God is operative in the universe . . . forever! The Lord Jesus meant what He said when He remarked, "And I give unto them *eternal* life; and they shall never perish."[3]

Another lesson we must learn is that the lasting quality of salvation is quite apart from circumstances. Peter wrote to people who were going through trials: "Ye greatly rejoice, though now for a season, if need be, ye are in heaviness through manifold temptations . . . That the trial of your faith . . . might be found unto praise and honor and glory at the appearing of Jesus Christ: whom having not seen, ye love; in whom, though now ye see him not, yet believing, ye rejoice with joy unspeakable and full of glory."[4]

Look closely at these words, "In whom . . . ye rejoice." The word *whom* refers to a Person, the Lord Jesus Christ. Put it this way, "In *him* . . . ye rejoice."

Happiness depends upon what happens — circumstances. When circumstances are adverse, I am unhappy. When they are favorable, I am happy.

Joy, however, according to this passage, can be had when circumstances are completely in reverse. Look at the circumstances and you get "heaviness . . . manifold temptations . . . trial of your faith." Look at Jesus, and you get "greatly rejoice . . . rejoice with joy unspeakable and full of glory!" Your joy is a Person, and will last as long as that Person lasts!

Furthermore, joy in Christ can make even unhappy circumstances serve you . . . work for your good. This is exactly what Paul says: "For our light affliction, which is but for a moment, worketh for us a far more exceeding and eternal weight of glory" (II Cor. 4:17).

"Worketh for us"—what works for me? Affliction — the very thing that had me scared . . . threatened to make me quit! God is making my enemy work for me!

The same truth is expressed in Romans 5 where Paul says: "We glory in tribulations also: knowing that *tribulation worketh* patience; and patience, experience; and experience, hope; and hope maketh not ashamed."[5]

Go a step farther and look at Romans 8:28: "And we know that all things work together for good to them that love God, to them who are the called according to his purpose." There's the glorious truth: Since you belong to Jesus Christ, and since your life now operates under His sovereignty, nothing can touch your life without working *for* you, producing good!

Do you dare to worry, when you know Almighty God is concerning Himself about your every experience?

SUBSISTENCE — OR GROWTH?

Everything depends upon where you place the emphasis in this matter. Inevitably, if you

seek merely to maintain what you now have —
hoard it, keep it, preserve it — you are going to
be disappointed. Any businessman knows
that when he comes to the place where he is
only holding on to the clients he has and not
getting any new business, he's through. So it
is in the Christian life. Peter says: "As newborn babes, desire the sincere milk of the
Word, that ye may grow thereby" (I Peter 2:2).
And "grow in grace, and in the knowledge of
our Lord and Saviour Jesus Christ."[6] Paul remarked to the Thessalonians that "your faith
groweth exceedingly."[7] He also besought
them to "increase more and more."[8] And the
Lord Jesus said to His disciples: "These things
have I spoken unto you, that my joy might
remain in you, and that your joy might be full
. . . these things I speak in the world, that they
might have my joy fulfilled in themselves."[9]

Put the emphasis where it belongs! Don't try
to "hold on" to Christian joy. Go on with
Christ in the Word, and joy will take care of
itself—you'll be full of joy, because you're
filled with *Him!*

Here is the heart of the matter: You're part of
an eternal purpose . . . you're linked with an
eternally lovely Person . . . you're experiencing
a lifelong process of growth in His grace.

Salvation is not something to be endured. Enjoy it, friend, enjoy it!

COORDINATE SCRIPTURE FOR CHAPTER 2

1.   And we know that all things work together for good to them that love God, to them who are the called according to *his* purpose.— Romans 8:28.

2.   According as he hath chosen us in him before the foundation of the world, that we should be holy and without blame before him in love.— Ephesians 1:4.

3.   And I give unto them eternal life: and they shall never perish, neither shall any *man* pluck them out of my hand.— John 10:28.

4.   Wherein ye greatly rejoice, though now for a season, if need be, ye are in heaviness through manifold temptations:
That the trial of your faith, being much more precious than of gold that perisheth though it be tried with fire, might be found unto praise and honor and glory at the appearing of Jesus Christ:
Whom having not seen, ye love; in whom, though now ye see *him* not, yet believing, ye rejoice with joy unspeakable and full of glory.— I Peter 1:6-8.

5. And not only *so*, but we glory in tribulations also: knowing that tribulation worketh patience;

And patience, experience; and experience, hope;

And hope maketh not ashamed; because the love of God is shed abroad in our hearts by the Holy Ghost, which is given unto us.— Romans 5:3-5.

6. But grow in grace, and *in* the knowledge of our Lord and Saviour Jesus Christ. To him *be* glory, both now and forever. Amen.— II Peter 3:18.

7. We are bound to thank God always for you, brethren, as it is meet, because that your faith groweth exceedingly, and the charity of every one of you all toward each other aboundeth.— II Thessalonians 1:3.

8. And indeed ye do it toward all the brethren which are in all Macedonia: but we beseech you, brethren, that ye increase more and more.— I Thessalonians 4:10.

9. And now come I to thee; and these things I speak in the world, that they might have my joy fulfilled in themselves.—John 17:13.

Well, I've started . . . wonder how long I can hold out. Folks claim it will "wear off," as they say. That makes religion sound like a hangover! I certainly know that there are some stiff battles on up ahead. I've got to make the grade somehow . . . nothing worse than to make this profession and then have to come crawling back to the old crowd to admit that I'm licked. I'll try—but is trying enough?

3

THE BATTLE AHEAD
or
What to Do in Temptation

The first thing to do about temptation is to expect it. There is nothing unusual or abnormal about being tempted. Rather, the person who is never tempted should question whether he is spiritually alive!

Let us get the proper approach to this matter. Not, "Why must I be tempted . . . go through all this testing?" Rather, "People *are* tempted: that much I know. I am not any different from other human beings, therefore I shall be tempted. What provision does God make for me?"

The Bible takes temptation for granted. Our Lord Jesus was "tempted in all points . . . like as we are."[1] He felt the mental anguish that temptation occasions, too, for we read "he himself hath suffered being tempted."[2]

James says that, rather than being thrown into a panic by it, we are to "count it all joy when ye fall into divers temptations" (Jas. 1:12), and Peter assures us that "the Lord knoweth how to deliver the godly out of temptations." [3]Paul remarks that your temptation is no different from the testing to which everyone else is subjected—"that which is common to man,"[4] and the Lord Jesus Christ teaches us as His disciples to pray, "Lead us not into temptation."[5]

The Devil's business is temptation. He tempted the Lord Jesus — in fact he is called the tempter in Matthew 4:3, and Paul calls Satan the tempter in writing to the Thessalonians.[6] Do you think the Devil is going out of business just because you were converted?

Learn to recognize temptation when it comes. James says that temptation is based upon desire: "Every man is tempted, when he is drawn away of his own lust [desire], and enticed" (Jas. 1:14).

Every one of us has certain natural desires — God made us that way. We desire food, fellowship, self-preservation, a sense of accomplishment — many other things. Then, because we are members of a sinful race, we have certain wrong desires — to cheat, and lie, and be avenged, and get the better of our fellowman. These good and evil desires are mixed together in the chemistry of your soul. Satan operates on the basis of using *what you already want* as a means of leading you into sin.

Of course it is simple enough to recognize temptation based upon wrong desires. If it's a wrong desire, it will lead to a wrong act and you know it. Never act upon a wrong desire — you will only get into more sin and trouble.

Not so easily identified, however, are temptations based upon good and legitimate desires. Remember at the very outset that Satan is interested in taking that which is good in your life and prostituting it to his own devilish ends. Here are a couple of questions that will help you settle the matter.

I am about to take this or that course of action. Does it glorify God?[7] Can I do it in the name of the Lord Jesus, and offer a prayer of thanksgiving over it?[8] Does it make me more preoccupied with "things," or does it help me in spending more time at the feet of Jesus?[9] Does it help to build up (edify) my Christian life, or does it tear down?[10] Will it offend another?[11]

If you will honestly ask these questions regarding any doubtful course of action, you will recognize temptation when it comes, and will be prepared to resist it in the power that Christ gives.

Having recognized temptation, the next thing is to resist it. Let us be honest about this business. The Christian faith is not an automatic cure-all for you. If you *want* to go on in sin you *will* go on in sin and nothing can stop you! Unless you want to be different, you never will be different. And until you desire victory over temptation enough to take a stand against it, you'll get exactly nowhere.

Search your heart today, remembering that it is "deceitful above all things, and desperately wicked,"[12] and find out the truth. Do I want victory over temptation and sin, or do I want an easy way to forgiveness and heaven, *while remaining in sin?*

Basically, taking your stand toward temptation is taking your stand with Christ. This is nothing new, because you did it when you came for salvation. You said, "When Christ died, I died *with* Him, because He was dying *for* me. When He rose, I rose *with* Him. Therefore, I trust Him as my Saviour, and identify myself with Him for salvation."[13] Now, as you face temptation, identify yourself afresh with your blessed Lord. Does He hate sin? Then so must you! Does He desire holiness of character and life? Then let that desire be fanned into flame in your soul. Gladden God's heart with a response like that of the little child. Seated at a restaurant table, faced with a choice from among a dozen possible items, she said simply, "Papa, I want what *you* want." "And because ye are sons, God hath sent forth the Spirit of his Son into your hearts, crying, Abba, Father" (Gal. 4:6).

Granted now that you are prepared to resist temptation because of being identified with Christ, never make the mistake of attempting it in your own strength. You started with Him—He did the saving work that made you a child of God. Don't leave Him now, and flounder about trying to keep yourself afloat. Well does Paul ask, "Having begun in the Spirit, are ye now made perfect by the flesh?" No, he says, "the just shall *live* by faith."[14] You started by faith—simply trusting Jesus. Now keep right on the same way!

See what the Word says about God, and temptation, and you. He knows how to deliver the godly out of temptation.[15] He knows how you feel, because He suffered, being tempted.[16] He will never allow you to be tested beyond your power to endure.[17] He encourages you to watch and pray that you enter not into temptation.[18] And He promises to keep you.[19]

Even more specifically, the business of the Lord Jesus Christ is to represent you—and your need—to God the Father. "Wherefore he is able also to save them to the uttermost that come unto God by him, seeing he ever liveth to make intercession for them" (Heb. 7:25).

He is able—because He is God.

To save—because He died for me.

To the uttermost—there will never be a situation, never a temptation, that He cannot handle.

He ever liveth to make intercession for them—day and night, the wounded hands of Jesus are stretched forth to God the Father in eloquent pleading . . . not only to save me, but to keep me as well!

We left out one phrase in the above breakdown. What was it? "Them . . . that come unto God by him." What kind of persons does the Lord Jesus help in temptation? Those that come to God and ask for help through Him!

God will never do the coming and the asking *for* you. Jesus died for you and now lives for you, but you must come for yourself.

If you are determined to resist temptation in the strength that God gives, come to the throne of grace and receive it! "Let us therefore come boldly unto the throne of grace, that we may obtain mercy, and find grace to help in time of need" (Heb. 4:16).

You should call for help NOW, when you need help. Too many times we make the mistake of postponing our praying. Later, too late, we pray sadly, "Lord, I failed. Please forgive and cleanse me." Now such praying is effective, and we shall speak of it in a moment, but is it not infinitely better to pray *now*, when I need help, and receive it? Our verse speaks of help "in time of need." Actually, this means "in the nick o'time."

> Just when I need Him most,
> Just when I need Him most;
> Jesus is near to comfort and cheer,
> Just when I need Him most!

It is important to recognize the place of the Word of God in helping you to meet temptation. You may be absolutely certain of this: The only thing you are *naturally* capable of is

41

sin and more sin; failure and more failure. Only the Word of God taking root in your life can change the natural into the supernatural. "Wherewithal shall a young man cleanse his way? By taking heed thereto according to thy word . . . Thy word have I hid in mine heart, that I might not sin against thee" (Ps. 119:9, 11). Paul speaks of "the washing of water by the word,"[20] and the Lord Jesus said, "Now ye are clean through the word which I have spoken unto you" (John 15:3).

Christ used the Word of God exclusively in dealing with Satan during the wilderness temptation.[21] To every leering suggestion of the Devil, our blessed Lord answered, "It is written . . ." After the final, triumphant Scripture, "It is written, thou shalt worship the Lord thy God, and him only shalt thou serve," we read, "Then the devil leaveth him." Hallelujah!

There is a Scripture answer to every suggestion Satan can ever make. Know the Word, and you'll know the sweet taste of victory over temptation.

Habit is important in dealing with temptation. Monotonously, you kept on failing before . . . now form the habit of bringing everything to Jesus, and make victory as habitual as failure ever was! Not by chance does the old song say,

> Each victory will help you
> Some other to win.

What if you fail? You are still quite capable of failure. Should it occur, confess your sin immediately, being explicit about it in prayer. The "Lord bless me" kind of prayer will not do here. It's "Lord, I lied," or "I cheated," or whatever may have occurred. "If we confess our sins, he is faithful and just to forgive us our sins, and to cleanse us from all unrighteousness" (I John 1:9).

Never let a day go by but that you are, as the old-timers used to say, "confessed and prayed up to date." That is what the Word of God calls "walking in the light." And "if we walk in the light as he is in the light, we have fellowship one with another, and the blood of Jesus Christ his Son cleanseth us from all sin" (I John 1:7).

You are ready now to deal with temptation. Expect it, recognize it, resist it, depend on God only, and use the Word.

1.   For we have not an high priest which cannot be touched with the feeling of our infirmities; but was in all points tempted like as *we are* yet without sin.— Hebrews 4:15.

2.   For in that he himself hath suffered being tempted, he is able to succor them that are tempted.— Hebrews 2:18.

3.   The Lord knoweth how to deliver the godly out of temptations, and to reserve the unjust unto the day of judgment to be punished.— II Peter 2:9.

4.   There hath no temptation taken you but such as is common to man: but God is faithful, who will not suffer you to be tempted above that ye are able; but will with the temptation also make a way to escape, that ye may be able to bear it.— I Corinthians 10:13.

5.   And lead us not into temptation, but deliver us from evil: For thine is the kingdom, and the power, and the glory, forever. Amen.— Matthew 6:13.

6.   For this cause, when I could no longer forbear, I sent to know your faith, lest by some means the tempter have tempted you, and our labor be in vain.— I Thessalonians 3:5.

7.   Whether therefore ye eat or drink, or what-soever ye do, do all to the glory of God.— I Corinthians 10:31.

8.   And whatsoever ye do in word or deed, *do* all in the name of the Lord Jesus, giving thanks to God and the Father by him.— Colossians 3:17.

9.   And the cares of this world, and the deceitfulness of riches, and the lusts of other things entering in, choke the word, and it becometh unfruitful.— Mark 4:19.

And Jesus answered and said unto her, Martha, Martha, thou art careful and troubled about many things.— Luke 10:41.

10.   How is it then, brethren? when ye come together, every one of you hath a psalm, hath doctrine, hath a tongue, hath a revelation, hath an interpretation. Let all things be done unto edifying.

All things are lawful for me, but all things are not expedient: all things are lawful for me, but all things edify not.— I Corinthians 14:26; 10:23.

11.   And through thy knowledge shall the weak brother perish, for whom Christ died?

But when ye sin so against the brethren, and wound their weak conscience, ye sin against Christ.

Wherefore, if meat make my brother to offend, I will eat no flesh while the world standeth, lest I make my brother to offend.— I Corinthians 8:11-13.

12. The heart *is* deceitful above all *things*, and desperately wicked: who can know it?— Jeremiah 17:9.

13. I am crucified with Christ: nevertheless I live; yet not I, but Christ liveth in me: and the life which I now live in the flesh I live by the faith of the Son of God, who loved me, and gave himself for me.— Galatians 2:20.

Therefore we are buried with him by baptism into death: that like as Christ was raised up from the dead by the glory of the Father, even so we also should walk in newness of life.

For if we have been planted together in the likeness of his death, we shall be also in the likeness of his resurrection.— Romans 6:4, 5.

14. Are ye so foolish? having begun in the Spirit, are ye now made perfect by the flesh?

But that no man is justified by the law in the sight of God, it is evident: for, The just shall live by faith.— Galatians 3:3, 11.

15. The Lord knoweth how to deliver the godly out of temptations, and to reserve the unjust unto the day of judgment to be punished.— II Peter 2:9.

16. For in that he himself hath suffered being tempted, he is able to succor them that are tempted.— Hebrews 2:18.

17.   There hath no temptation taken you but such as is common to man: but God is faithful, who will not suffer you to be tempted above that ye are able; but will with the temptation also make a way to escape, that ye may be able to bear it.— I Corinthians 10:13.

18.   Watch and pray, that ye enter not into temptation: the spirit indeed is willing, but the flesh is weak.— Matthew 26:41.

19.   Because thou hast kept the word of my patience, I also will keep thee from the hour of temptation, which shall come upon all the world, to try them that dwell upon the earth.— Revelation 3:10.

To an inheritance incorruptible, and undefiled, and that fadeth not away, reserved in heaven for you,

Who are kept by the power of God through faith unto salvation ready to be revealed in the last time.

Wherein ye greatly rejoice, though now for a season, if need be, ye are in heaviness through manifold temptations.— I Peter 1:4-6.

20.   That he might sanctify and cleanse it with the washing of water by the word.— Ephesians 5:26.

21.   Then was Jesus led up of the spirit into the wilderness to be tempted of the devil. And when he had fasted forty days and forty nights, he was afterward an hungered.

And when the tempter came to him, he said, If thou be the Son of God, command that these stones be made bread. But he answered and said, It is written, Man shall not live by bread alone, but by every word that proceedeth out of the mouth of God.

Then the devil taketh him up into the holy city, and setteth him on a pinnacle of the temple,

And saith unto him, If thou be the Son of God, cast thyself down: for it is written, He shall give his angels charge concerning thee: and in their hands they shall bear thee up, lest at any time thou dash thy foot against a stone.

Jesus said unto him. It is written again, Thou shalt not tempt the Lord thy God.

Again, the devil taketh him up into an exceeding high mountain, and sheweth him all the kingdoms of the world, and the glory of them;

And saith unto him, All these things will I give thee, if thou wilt fall down and worship me.

Then saith Jesus unto him, Get thee hence, Satan: for it is written, Thou shalt worship the Lord thy God, and him only shalt thou serve.

Then the devil leaveth him, and, behold, angels came and ministered unto him.— Matthew 4:1-11.

*People confuse me . . . some say "Do," others,
"Don't." Some have extremely high standards and are
utterly devoted to Christ, while others are not so strict,
but seem to love the Lord just as much. After whom do I
pattern . . . where, and how, do I start to . . . act like a
Christian?*

4

HOW DO I ACT LIKE A CHRISTIAN?
or
Wanted: A Christian Character

START WITH A PERSON

The Christian life has always been a mystery to the unsaved. Paul says the unsaved man cannot receive "the things of the Spirit of God: for they are foolishness unto him: neither can he know them, because they are spiritually discerned."[1] It need not be a mystery to you, however, for it is now "made manifest to his saints: to whom God would make known what is the riches of the glory of this mystery among the Gentiles; which is *Christ in you*, the hope of glory."[2]

This whole truth becomes embarrassingly

simple, once you see through it. A *Person* saved you, did He not? And it takes a *Person* to keep you day by day.

"I need Thee every hour — stay Thou near by!

Temptations lose their power when Thou art nigh."

Well then, in this matter of producing a Christian character, what makes you think *you* can do it? The blessed Son of God now dwells in you, and it is He who now controls the development of your life.

The secret of Christian character is . . . Jesus Christ! Living within and living out through you, *His* life becomes apparent, where once only your failures were seen. This is what Paul means when he exclaims:[3] "Christ liveth in me: and the life which I now live in the flesh I live by the faith of the Son of God."

SURRENDER TO A PERSON

The Lord Jesus Christ dwells in your heart by His Spirit, but He will control only that portion of your life which you yield to Him. This is the reason behind Paul's words: "I beseech you therefore, brethren, by the mercies of God, that ye present your bodies a living sacrifice, holy, acceptable unto God, which is your reasonable service."[4]

Present what?

Your body.

Why?

Because His Spirit now dwells in your body, and the only way He can express His life and love is through a yielded instrument. Don't expect the Holy Spirit to transform your heart-house if you refuse to let Him into all the rooms in it! Because you're a Christian, you have a right to all of the Holy Spirit as your birthright;[5] but the big question now is: Does He have all of you?

This need not be a painful experience, or something which you must necessarily seek. Right now, if you mean business with God about it, you can bow your head, and give over to God the Holy Spirit complete control of yourself — body, soul, and spirit. That is the first step in developing Christian character. Only *He* can develop it, so start by letting *Him* take control.

One big surprise you'll meet about this time is that the things for which you sought so eagerly along the line of Christian character — things like a loving heart, a generous disposition, and a faithful performance of duty — are not an end in themselves, but a result!

The passage that presents this truth is Galatians 5:22, 23. Look it up, and read, first of all, the three verses which precede this passage. "Works of the flesh" is the ugly title. We ought constantly to remind ourselves that all the flesh — our old Adam nature — is capable of, is dead works; actually, a perversion of the good which we seek — every item on that heartbreaking list is a twisted, perverted opposite of some virtue.

"But," he says, "the fruit of the Spirit is love, joy, peace. . . ."

Fruit, did you say, Paul?

Yes, fruit.

But why change the figure of speech, Paul? You were speaking of the works of the flesh in those three preceding verses. Should you not now speak of the works of the Spirit?

The aged apostle is silent a moment. No, he says, not works, for the Christian life is not mechanical, but vital. The life of the Holy Spirit unites with your life, and produces a life product. Christian character is never primarily the things you do — it's the person you are, as a result of being indwelt by *the* Person — the Holy Spirit.

COMMUNE WITH A PERSON

The word "communion," when applied to our relationship to God in developing Christian character, has two phases. You'll find them outlined in Philippians 4:6-8.

Paraphrasing Paul's words, we read: Don't worry about anything; pray about everything, and God will give you that miraculous, perfect peace that the world envies but only Christians possess.

The first phase of communion is to *take everything you know about yourself to Him.* "Everything by prayer and supplication." There is absolutely nothing about which you dare not pray. God is GOD — great enough to run the universe and still have time for the most minute detail of your life.

Tell the truth: There are still many things in your life *about which you know*, but which you have never voiced to God in prayer. Either carelessness, or fear, has kept you from it. Simply, the truth is this: If you want to be different, tell Jesus about it.

The second phase of communion is to *take everything you know about Him . . . to yourself!* You may not realize it, but verse eight is a perfect description of Jesus Christ: "What-

soever things are true [Rev. 3:7] . . .[6] honest
[John 8:45] . . .[7] just [Matt. 27:19] . . .[8] pure [I
John 3:3] . . .[9] lovely [Song of Sol. 5:16] . . .[10] of
good report [Mark 7:37] . . .[11] virtue [Mark
5:30] . . .[12] praise [I Pet. 4:11]."[13] Now . . . all
these things that He is . . . THINK on these
things . . . take them to yourself . . . make them
part of your life, by faith!

OBEY A PERSON

"Whatsoever he saith unto you, do it,"[14]
Wisehearted Mary! She knew the secret of success when dealing with our blessed Lord. So
did Paul. If you'll turn again to that passage in
Philippians 4, you will find him saying in
verse 9: "Those things, which ye have both
learned, and received, and heard, and seen in
me, do: and the God of peace shall be with
you."

By now you are familiar with the process by
which one finds out what God wants him to
do. Here it is, carefully delineated for you:

Learned — gained from reading the Word.

Received — gained from experience with
God.

Heard — gained from exhortation from the
servant of God.

Seen in me — gained from observation of true Christian character in others.

What now? Look carefully at the next word, "Do." God will never force you to obey. There comes a time when, after His Spirit has dealt with you, and His Word has informed you, that you must *act*; either to obey, or to disobey. Obey Him, and you'll experience the blessed fulfillment of the promise given only to those who obey, "The God of peace shall be with you." We receive the peace of God when we pray about everything and commit it to Him. But we know the precious awareness of the presence of God only when we obey Him! A number of scriptures prove this point. Peter, bold in his new experience of the Holy Spirit's power said: "And we are witnesses of these things; and so is also the Holy Ghost, whom God hath given to them that obey him" (Acts 5:32). Peter *received* the Holy Ghost in answer to the promise of the Father, according to the Word of the Lord Jesus, but he was *aware* of the Holy Ghost, because he was just then obeying God.

Again, in Matthew 28:19, 20, we hear the Lord Jesus saying, "Go ye . . ." — a definite command. Then, presupposing their obedience, He says, "and lo, I am with you alway, even unto the end of the world."

Friend, when God is with you — because you are surrendered to Him, communing with Him, obeying Him — *you'll be different*, and the people will know it. Read I Samuel 3:19, 20.

IMPORTANT COUNSEL

Major on spirituality. Look for the things, the people, the associations in life that will make you more effective as a Christian. Better be ignorant on some of the news of the day, if you must, rather than miss being the bearer of good news from heaven. Make the rule of your life Philippians 3:10 — to know Him, to share His heart, to resemble Him, with the mark of the cross upon you!

Expect people to fail, then they won't disappoint you when they do. By this we mean not cynicism, but an awareness of the fact that Romans 3:23 is absolutely true, all the time. Never hitch your wagon to any earthly star — it will some day flicker and go out. People — the best people — fail sometimes, but Jesus never fails. "Looking unto Jesus, the author and finisher of our faith!"

Always choose the high road when faced with a choice between two courses of conduct. If

58

there's a better, holier, purer, more generous, more honest way to do anything—take that way!

If there's any doubt about a thing, it's wrong for you. Someone else may do it with a perfectly clear conscience. Let him. If *you* are in doubt, don't touch it. "Whatsoever is not of faith is sin."[15] That means: Whatever you can't be absolutely sure is the will of God, that's wrong. Stay away from it.

Position as a Christian among other Christians depends squarely on your passion for Christ. Strive not to be like brother or sister So-and-so, but to be more like Christ . . . to love Him more devotedly, and serve Him more faithfully. You'll rate as a Christian in direct proportion to how much—or how little —Christ dominates your life.

The true Christian is the one who lives his love for Christ all the time. Real love refuses to be pigeonholed! Either it affects all that you are and do, or it is no love at all. Right now, get on your knees, and stay there until you can honestly answer the question of John 21:15—"Lovest thou me . . . more . . . ?" When you love Him supremely, you'll serve Him acceptably. Then, Christian character will be, not a trial, but a triumph—His triumph!

COORDINATE SCRIPTURE FOR
CHAPTER 4

1.   But the natural man receiveth not the things of the Spirit of God: for they are foolishness unto him: neither can he know *them,* because they are spiritually discerned.—I Corinthians 2:14.

2.   *Even* the mystery which hath been hid from ages and from generations, but now is made manifest to his saints:
   To whom God would make known what *is* the riches of the glory of this mystery among the Gentiles; which is Christ in you, the hope of glory.—Colossians 1:26, 27.

3.   I am crucified with Christ: nevertheless I live; yet not I, but Christ liveth in me: and the life which I now live in the flesh, I live by the faith of the Son of God, who loved me, and gave himself for me.—Galatians 2:20.

4.   I beseech you therefore, brethren, by the mercies of God, that ye present your bodies a living sacrifice, acceptable unto God, *which is* your reasonable service.— Romans 12:1.

5.   But ye are not in the flesh, but in the Spirit, if so be that the Spirit of God dwell in you. Now if any man have not the Spirit of Christ, he is none of his.— Romans 8:9.

What! know ye not that your body is the temple of the Holy Ghost *which is* in you, which ye have of God, and ye are not your own?

For ye are bought with a price: therefore glorify God in your body, and in your spirit, which are God's.— I Corinthians 6:19, 20.

6.   And to the angel of the church in Philadelphia write: These things saith he that is holy, he that is true, he that hath the key of David, he that openeth, and no man shutteth; and shutteth, and no man openeth.— Revelation 3:7.

7.   And because I tell *you* the truth, ye believe me not.— John 8:45.

8.   When he was set down on the judgment seat, his wife sent unto him, saying, Have thou nothing to do with that just man; for I have suffered many things this day in a dream because of him.— Matthew 27:19.

9.   And every man that hath this hope in him purifieth himself, even as he is pure.— I John 3:3.

10.   His mouth *is* most sweet; yea, he *is* altogether lovely. This *is* most sweet; yea, he *is* altogether lovely. This *is* my beloved, and this *is* my friend, O daughters of Jerusalem.— Song of Solomon 5:16.

11.   And were beyond measure astonished, saying, He hath done all things well: he maketh both

the deaf to hear, and the dumb to speak.— Mark 7:37.

12. And Jesus, immediately knowing in himself that virtue had gone out of him, turned him about in the press, and said, Who touched my clothes?— Mark 5:30.

13. If any man speak, *let him speak* as the oracles of God; if any man minister, *let him do it* as of the ability which God giveth: that God in all things may be glorified through Jesus Christ, to whom be praise and dominion forever and ever. Amen.— I Peter 4:11.

14. His mother saith unto the servants, Whatsoever he saith unto you, do it.— John 2:5.

15. And he that doubteth is damned if he eat, because he eateth not of faith: for whatsoever is not of faith is sin.— Romans 14:23.

Therefore to him that knoweth to do good, and doeth it not, to him it is sin.— James 4:17.

Christians venerate the Bible — that is no surprise to me. What I can't understand is that so many of them enjoy reading it, talk familiarly of its truths, and really know their way around in its pages. Because I'm now a Christian, I want to have a Christian attitude toward the Word of God, but where do I start reading, how do I study it — in other words, what's the secret that will make the Bible really interesting?

5

WHAT TO DO ABOUT THE BIBLE
or
Holy Book . . . Living Guide: Which?

You already have within you the secret of interest in the Bible. Whether you know it or not, you will always be hungry for the Word of God . . . because you're a Christian! The person who is right with God instinctively loves His Word. "O how love I thy law!" exclaimed the psalmist. "It is my meditation all the day . . . How sweet are thy words unto my taste! Yea, sweeter than honey to my mouth!" (Ps. 119:97, 103).

If "Christ in you, the hope of glory," is the secret of Christian assurance and character, it is also the basic provision for your success with the Word. The *Living Word* now dwells in your heart by faith, and His Spirit reminds you moment by moment of your need for the written Word. The Lord Jesus was speaking expressly of your need for the Bible's life-giving truth when He said that the Holy Spirit would "bring all things to your remembrance, whatsoever I have said unto you" (John 14:26).

Your business now is to recognize that God has put this holy hunger for the Word in your heart; to know that you will never be satisfied with anything *less* than the Word of God, and to make daily provision for generous portions of the Living Bread.

SOME THINGS YOU SHOULD KNOW

Help yourself to a blessing right here, by going over some of the things the Bible does for God's children.

We grow by the Word of God. "As newborn babes," says Peter, "desire the sincere milk of the word, that ye may grow thereby: if so be ye have tasted that the Lord is gracious" (I Pet. 2:2, 3). Are you recently saved? Then you're a babe in Christ, and your first need is to grow. Christians grow through feeding on the Word. More later in this chapter about *how* to do it.

We are changed by the Word. "But we all, with open face beholding as in a glass [the Bible is God's heavenly looking glass where we see reflected our needs and His glory] the glory of the Lord, are changed into the same image from glory to glory, even as by the Spirit of the Lord" (II Cor. 3:18). Would you be more like Jesus? Read the Bible!

We are cleansed by the Word. "Wherewithal shall a young man cleanse his way? by taking heed thereto according to thy word (Ps. 119:9).[1]

We are kept by the Word. "Thy word have I hid in mine heart, that I might not sin against thee" (Ps. 119:11).

We share God's life through the Word. "The words that I speak unto you, they are spirit, and they are life."[2]

We defeat the Devil through the Word. "And they overcame him by the blood of the Lamb, *and by the word* of their testimony; and they loved not their lives unto the death" (Rev. 12:11). "The sword of the Spirit, which is the word of God" (Eph. 6:17).

We win souls through preaching the Word. Christ "preached the word unto them."[3] The early church preached the Word.[4] God promises to bless His Word — not your opinions.

We base our faith on the Word, *and produce faith* in others by proclaiming the Word.[5]

Our eternal authority is the Word,[6] therefore we speak confidently and authoritatively as did the prophets when they said, "Thus saith the Lord."

Every needed blessing is in the Word.[7] Here are just a few from Psalm 119: Cleansing, quickening, strengthening, establishing, comfort, hope, guidance, order, pleasant meditation, joy, understanding, deliverance. You need never lack for anything while you have the Word of God!

SOME THINGS YOU SHOULD DO

Cultivate a regard for the Bible as being literally The . . . Word . . . of . . . God. No longer merely a holy book, it must now become the very stuff of which your moral and spiritual fabric is woven. When you were unsaved, you could quibble about whether or not the Word was important. Now . . . that point is forever settled. It *is* God's Word — treat it as such.

Get a good Bible, with readable print. Nothing discourages the beginner more than having to struggle with sticking pages and fine type. Your eyes blur, your mind grows weary; and before you realize it, the Devil has won another victory. Get a good Bible! The money you invest in it will be repaid times without number.

Make up your mind that you are going to read your Bible every day from now until you get to Glory. You expect to eat pretty regularly until you leave this world, don't you? Let's have as much sense about our spiritual condition as we try to show in maintaining our physical bodies! Believe me, friend, many a life has been wrecked by neglect of this truth: You cannot live successfully and forget the Bible. You *must* feed your soul![8]

Learn to *eat* the Word of God. Jeremiah says: "Thy words were found, and I did eat them; and thy word was unto me the joy and rejoicing of mine heart: for I am called by thy name, O Lord God of hosts" (Jer. 15:16). How do you eat the Word? Well, what happens when you take physical food into your body? That little boy drinks a glass of milk. His body takes white milk, and turns it into white teeth, and blue eyes and yellow hair, and strong bones, and a clear, ruddy complexion. What he eats becomes part of his life.

Here's how to eat the Word: Take your Bible and open it to the book through which you happen to be reading. Get on your knees, and ask God in Jesus' name to speak to you from His Word. Read, and reread the passage until, in the stillness of your heart, God the Holy

Spirit says something . . . from the Word . . . just for you! When He does, get paper and a pen and write it down. Now, still on your knees before God, pray back to Him what He said to your heart. Pray, on the basis of God's Word to you, until your very soul is aflame with the message. Then arise and proceed to put into action that which God has put into your life. Share with someone as soon as possible the blessings you received through eating the Word.

Make a time each day when you will read the Word of God, the earlier in your day the better. The longer you put off getting into the Word, the less value in eternity will your day have. And be very sure, if you do not make a place for the Word, you will never have a consistent Christian life. Invariably the up-and-then-down-ers, the feeble brethren and sisters who never make the grade for God, are the folk who either willfully, or stupidly, refuse to make a place and time in their daily schedule for God's Word.

Everything in the Bible has some connection with the Lord Jesus and His work for, in, and through the believer. Always read your Bible with this in mind: How will I find Christ revealed in the Word today?

Read the Bible sensibly, as you would a textbook.

Read it earnestly, as a lawyer scans a contract: each word was put into the Bible by the Holy Spirit and has its own definite meaning for you.

Read God's Word ardently, as a lover reads a love letter. The Bible is God's love letter to you: "Yea, I have loved thee with an everlasting love," He says. "Therefore with loving kindness have I drawn thee" (Jer. 31:3).

When you have read it, speak enthusiastically of the Bible to your friends and acquaintances. Nothing is more conducive to joy and real growth in grace than speaking out that which you learned in the secret place.

Start reading and studying the easier portions of the Bible first. The Gospel of John, for instance, was expressly written to lead folk to Christ (John 20:31) and presents Him in a most wonderful manner. The Book of Acts tells how the early church was formed and how any normal church operates; tells of missionary endeavors, and creates a soul-winner's vision in the hearts of those who read it. The Book of Romans breaks down in detail the truth of the Gospel—*why* you need a Saviour, *how* you are saved, and *what* happens after you are saved.

This will give you a start. After that, you're on your own!

Build your life around the Bible. NOTHING WILL EVER BE SO IMPORTANT TO YOU AS THE WORD OF GOD! No other book, magazine, newspaper, activity, recreation, friend or loved one, will ever have the right to demand so much, or the power to contribute so much in your life as the Scriptures.

Neglect the Bible, and you neglect your own soul. Read and obey it, and you enhance your own life while blessing countless others.

HOW TO "BREAK OPEN" THE WORD OF GOD

Always—ALWAYS—begin your Bible study with earnest prayer for God's enlightenment and guidance: "Open thou mine eyes, that I may behold wondrous things out of thy law" (Ps. 119:18). The Holy Spirit takes time to say that "the natural man receiveth not the things of the Spirit of God," and "they that are in the flesh cannot please God," and "without faith it is impossible to please him." So if you would have God's approval on your Bible study, better come to Him first in prayer about it.

Remember that the main subject of the Bible

is redemption . . . and that the main Person of redemption is the Lord Jesus Christ. Sensible Bible study, then, will *look for references to Him* in every page of Holy Writ. In the Old Testament, you will find Him pictured in ritual (Tabernacle and Levitical sacrifices), in types (people who foreshadowed Christ by their lives), and in prophetic truth (utterances which point directly to either the first or second coming of Christ).

In the New Testament, you will see the various aspects of His ministry beautifully depicted by the varying approaches of the Gospels. W. H. Griffith Thomas says: "We may consider four passages beginning with 'Behold' and note:

a) Behold a King. Isa. 32:1 (Matthew)
b) Behold My Servant. Isa. 42:1 (Mark)
c) Behold the Man. John 19:5 (Luke)
d) Behold your God. Isa. 40:9 (John)[9]

"The aim is one and the same, but their methods and aspects differ. St. Matthew demonstrates; St. Mark depicts; St. Luke declares; St. John describes. St. Matthew demonstrates (based on Old Testament) the coming of an expected Saviour; St. Mark depicts the life of a powerful Saviour; St. Luke declares the grace of a human Saviour; St. John describes the possession of a personal Saviour."*

Everything in the Bible has its own beautiful relationship to our Lord Jesus Christ: "Beginning at Moses and all the prophets, he expounded unto them in all the scriptures the things concerning himself" (Luke 24:27).

Here are some other things you will find helpful in your reading and study of God's Word:

1. Read entire books of the Bible, and find their main theme and message.

2. Follow individual life stories in the Bible, and you will discover some most fascinating biography.

3. Follow through the development of a truth or a doctrine. Mark with a certain color, for instance, every verse that deals with God's grace, or His love.

4. Look for casual references to people — references that give an index to their character. Of Absalom, for example, all the Holy Spirit could say was that he was handsome, had beautiful hair, and cut it once a year! (II Sam. 14:25, 26). What an indication of supreme vanity.

---

*Methods of Bible Study, by W. H. Griffith Thomas.

5. Look for verbs denoting action. After your first casual reading of a passage, go back and underscore all the words that denote action of any kind. You will be amazed by the clarity of the message thus relayed.

6. Read and reread a chapter until you are able to pick out its theme, topic sentence, best verse, and lasting lesson. Anywhere from six to twenty readings are indicated here, but when you're through, you'll have the chapter, and it will have you!

7. Remember: ALWAYS FIND OUT WHAT THE BIBLE SAYS BEFORE YOU TRY TO TELL WHAT IT MEANS. Generally, when you know what the Word says about any given question, you will have no uncertainty over your own course of conduct.

SUPREMELY IMPORTANT

You must — YOU MUST — resolve to obey the Word as you read it. Just as neglect of the Word can cut the throat of your Christian endeavor, so a disobedient heart and mind will tune out heaven's message and leave only the static of your own mental meanderings. "Ye are my friends," Jesus said, "if ye do whatsoever I command you" (John 15:14). "We are his witnesses," said Peter, " and so is also the

Holy Ghost, whom God hath given *to them that obey him*" (Acts 5:32). Let your daily prayer be, "Lord, while I read Thy Word, give me wisdom to understand (Jas. 1:5) and grace and courage to obey!"

COORDINATE SCRIPTURE FOR CHAPTER 5

1. Now ye are clean through the word which I have spoken unto you.— John 15:3.

That he might sanctify and cleanse it with the washing of the water by the word.— Ephesians 5:26.

2. It is the spirit that quickeneth; the flesh profiteth nothing: the words that I speak unto you, they are spirit, and they are life.— John 6:63.

3. And straightway many were gathered together, insomuch that there was no room to receive them, no, not so much as about the door: and he preached the word unto them.— Mark 2:2.

4. And they, when they had testified and preached the word of the Lord, returned to Jerusalem, and preached the gospel in many villages of the Samaritans.— Acts 8:25.

And when they were at Salamis, they preached

the word of God in the synagogues of the Jews: and they had also John to their minister.— Acts 13:5.

And when they had preached the word in Perga, they went down into Attalia.— Acts 14:25.

5.   So then faith cometh by hearing, and hearing by the word of God.— Romans 10:17.

6.   Forever, O Lord, thy word is settled in heaven.— Psalm 119:89.

7.   According as his divine power hath given unto us all things that pertain unto life and godliness, through the knowledge of him that hath called us to glory and virtue:

Whereby are given unto us exceeding great and precious promises: that by these ye might be partakers of the divine nature, having escaped the corruption that is in the world through lust.— II Peter 1:3, 4.

8.   As newborn babes, desire the sincere milk of the word, that ye may grow thereby.— I Peter 2:2.

9.   Behold, a king shall reign in righteousness, and princes shall rule in judgment.— Isaiah 32:1.

Behold my servant, whom I uphold; mine elect, in whom my soul delighteth; I have put my spirit upon him: he shall bring forth judgment to the Gentiles.— Isaiah 42:1.

Then came Jesus forth, wearing the crown of thorns, and the purple robe. And Pilate saith unto them, Behold the man!— John 19:5.

O Zion, that bringest good tidings, get thee up into the high mountains; O Jerusalem, that bringest good tidings, lift up thy voice with strength; lift it up, be not afraid; say unto the cities of Judah, Behold your God!— Isaiah 40:9.

Prayer mystifies me. Some seem to agonize in prayer . . . others are quiet in their devotions. Some have a set form of approach to God, others are most informal in their address to the Deity. Some speak of "praying through," while others calmly say that they commit everything to the Lord.

Loud or soft . . . short or long . . . agony or litany — where do I fit in?

6

HOW CAN I PRAY?

Emphatically, prayer is *not* a polite speech to the Deity. One is convinced that when the books are opened, many a humanly acceptable prayer will be found among the "wood, hay, stubble"[1] because it was merely the effort of the flesh to cultivate favor with God.

WHAT PRAYER IS

Prayer is a cry. The physician expects the newborn babe to cry out, as first evidence of life. If it does not cry, he shakes or spanks it to produce a cry. If it continues silent, it will soon be dead.

Here is a singular thing. Peter says that we are "newborn babes"[2] and yet we never expect new converts to do the very thing that a babe ought to do: cry. "Because ye are sons," says

Paul, "God hath sent forth the Spirit of his Son into your hearts, crying, Abba, Father" (Gal. 4:6). *Abba* is the orientalism for our word "papa." It is the cry of a childlike heart that does not know much, but knows it is alive and that it needs the tender care of its heavenly Father.

Again, Paul says, "For ye have not received the spirit of bondage again to fear; but ye have received the Spirit of adoption, whereby we cry, Abba, Father" (Rom. 8:15).

God respects the cry of the converted heart. There are literally hundreds of references proving this fact. Here are a couple: "He shall deliver the needy when he crieth; the poor also, and him that hath no helper" (Ps. 72:12). "This poor man cried, and the Lord heard him, and saved him out of all his troubles" (Ps. 34:6).

I cannot speak strongly enough about this matter. Your birthright as a Christian is that warm, tender heart toward God . . . that cry down deep in your spirit that reaches its poor mute hands out to God and pleads more eloquently than the best of human words. Cherish that cry. Let it come out. Let it make itself heard in every one of your prayers, either private or public. Let us have done with cold, formal, heartless, pagan praying. It grieves the heart of God and leaves our own lives more poverty-stricken than they were before.

Do you know what that cry is? It is the blessed Holy Spirit in your heart, calling out to God. Because you *are* a Christian, He indwells you.[3] And because you frequently do not know what to say, He says it for you in the language that God Almighty understands. Look at these beautiful words: "Likewise the Spirit also helpeth our infirmities: for we know not what we should pray for as we ought: but the Spirit himself maketh intercession for us with groanings which cannot be uttered. And he that searcheth the hearts knoweth what is the mind of the Spirit, because he maketh intercession for the saints according to the will of God" (Rom. 8:26, 27).

Let us look honestly at this matter. You are newly converted — a babe in Christ. Sure, you don't know what to say, or how to say it. But deep within you there dwells One who does know, and whose business it is to express the very yearnings of the heart of God through your heart. That's the cry . . . the cry of the Holy Spirit. Prayer is a cry — His cry — to God through you!

Humanly speaking, prayer is often simply a call for help. "Call unto me, and I will answer thee, and show thee great and mighty things, which thou knowest not" (Jer. 33:3), is our encouragement.

A call means earnest desire, specific desire, determined and oftentimes desperate desire — and, thank God, a call to Him means an answer. "And it shall come to pass, that whosoever shall call on the name of the Lord shall be delivered . . . for whosoever shall call upon the name of the Lord shall be saved (Joel 2:32; Rom. 10:13).

Form the habit of calling upon God at every occasion of need in your life. A bowed head, an open heart, and the simple words, "Lord Jesus, help me now!" can mean the difference between defeat and victory.

Prayer involves confession and cleansing. "If I regard iniquity in my heart, the Lord will not hear me," said the psalmist soberly (Ps. 66:18). Isaiah sounds the same warning: "Behold, the Lord's hand is not shortened, that it cannot save; neither his ear heavy, that it cannot hear: but your iniquities have separated between you and your God, and your sins have hid his face from you, that he will not hear" (Isa. 59:1, 2).

Make up your mind to this now: I can never

hide known sin in my heart and expect to get my prayers answered.

Do you know how to get rid of sin? Confess it and forsake it. "He that covereth his sins shall not prosper: but whoso confesseth and forsaketh them shall have mercy" (Prov. 28:13). "If we confess our sins, he is faithful and just to forgive us our sins, and to cleanse us from all unrighteousness" (I John 1:9). Just tell God the truth about your sin: "Lord, I lied, or I cheated, or I stole, or I lost my temper." Specific confession will bring specific cleansing. (And, of course, when you have sinned against an individual, you'll go get right with that person, too.)

Like everything else in the Christian life, prayer must be Christ-centered. The disciples, beginners in the school of prayer, were told: "Hitherto have ye asked nothing in my name: ask, and ye shall receive, that your joy may be full" (John 16:24). Why is this? Look at the preceding verse: "Verily, verily, I say unto you, Whatsoever ye shall ask the Father in my name, he will give it you."

"In Jesus' name," we say when we pray — why?

Because that is the saving Name: "And thou

shalt call his name Jesus, for he shall save his people from their sins" (Matt. 1:21).

Because He is the only one through whom you can come to God: "No man cometh unto the Father, but by me," He said.[4]

Because He is the one whose work it is today tenderly to represent you in the Father's presence: "Wherefore he is able also to save them to the uttermost that come unto God by him, seeing he ever liveth to make intercession for them" (Heb. 7:25).

If Christ is the "everything" of salvation and life — and He is! — then He must also be the very heart of all your praying. Pray with a deep dependence on your living Lord and Intercessor, and you will always touch the heart of God.

THINGS TO REMEMBER

1. Have a time and place for daily prayer. Someone has well said, "If you do not have a time for prayer, you will soon not have time for prayer!" There is some place in your home, even though it be just a coal shed or a clothes closet, where you can get alone with God. Don't worry about discomfort — you pray better when you are not so comfortable as to be half asleep. Remember, Jonah prayed effec-

86

tively even in the belly of the whale. Location is relatively unimportant, but a definite time and place are all-important.

2. Have a prayer list — an agenda of things you want from God. Help yourself to a blessing and increasing richness of life by writing down the things you need from heaven's storehouse. Then go after them, one by one, earnestly, in faith, and in complete dependence upon your Lord. Save that list, and check off the answers when they come. You'll receive a real thrill when you are able to write "Hallelujah" and the date, beside some glorious answer to prayer on your prayer list. Always remember James 5:16-18. Elijah — an ordinary man, beset by ordinary temptations, but with a real faith in an Almighty God, prayed earnestly . . . and got an answer. He prayed again . . . and God answered again. No coincidence here — just a commonplace person praying to a mighty God.

3. Pray on the basis of God's Word. "And this is the confidence that we have in him, that, if we ask any thing according to his will, he heareth us: and if we know that he hear us, whatsoever we ask, we know that we have the petitions that we desired of him" (I John 5:14, 15).

Anything according to His will — where do you find the will of God? In His Word, of course. Search the Word of God until you find your own peculiar "praying ground" — a promise or a portion that is particularly applicable to your case — then pray on the authority and basis of that scripture. Friend, the answers will come trooping down from the throne of grace!

4. Maintain a quiet time daily with God. This involves bowing quietly and asking for consecration on the Word . . . reading until God speaks definitely to YOU . . . writing down what He said (if you can't write it succinctly, you haven't got it!) . . . then praying it back to Him: "This, Lord, is what Thou didst say to me." One more thing: Share what God said to you with someone else as quickly as you can. Praying it and telling it will fasten the truth in your heart and character.

5. Avoid forms and habitual expressions in prayer. Remember you are talking to a wonderful PERSON. Think how embarrassed you would be if you followed the "dear heavenly Father" repetition idea in speaking to a neighbor: "Good morning, dear Mr. Jones. How are you, dear Mr. Jones? Nice day, dear Mr. Jones,

etc., etc." There is no substitute for sense, courtesy, and thought in prayer.

6. Make prayer the springboard for obedience. Nothing will stultify your prayer life so much as the unwillingness to do what God whispers to your heart while you wait before Him. "But be ye doers of the word, and not hearers only, deceiving your own selves" (Jas. 1:22).

7. Look for an answer after you have prayed. Classic example of this truth is found in I Kings 18:41-46. Elijah . . . the victory on Mount Carmel . . . the promise of rain . . . the ground still parched and dry while the sun blazed down overhead. Elijah goes to prayer. While he prays, he sends his servant to look toward the sea. "And he went up and looked, and said, There is nothing. And he said, Go again seven times. And it came to pass at the seventh time, that he said, Behold there ariseth a little cloud out of the sea, like a man's hand . . . and it came to pass in the meanwhile, that the heaven was black with clouds and wind, and there was a great rain."

Faith is just expecting God to act like God! Elijah had prayed, and now he expected a God-like answer. Simple . . . keep praying and expecting until the answer arrives!

8. Never quit. God likes to have His people "that make mention of the Lord, keep not silence and give him no rest."[5] The Lord Jesus said, "Men ought always to pray, and not to faint."[6] Paul said, "Praying always,"[7] and, "Pray without ceasing" (I Thess. 5:17).

Never stop praying when you feel like stopping — Satan is just tempting you and trying to cheat you of a blessing. The time when you feel the weakest, and the most helpless, and when you realize that you are praying so poorly — THAT IS THE TIME TO KEEP ON. YOU ARE JUST ON THE THRESHOLD OF BLESSING! Pray through. Pray until the Holy Spirit has told you in your heart of hearts that God has heard and will answer. Then rise, praise Him, and expect the answer. It will come.

9. Expect the Holy Spirit to pray through *your* personality — not someone else. Never try to pray like another person. If you do, you will turn out to be nothing but a pious fraud. Avoid "ministerial tones" and the "pious whine" like the plague. Strive to be perfectly natural, utterly sincere, and completely yielded to the blessed Spirit of God. Then, no matter what form your prayer assumes, it will

really be YOU praying in the power of the Spirit.

COORDINATE SCRIPTURE FOR
CHAPTER 6

1.   Now if any man build upon this foundation gold, silver, precious stones, wood, hay, stubble;
    Every man's work shall be made manifest.— I Corinthians 3:12, 13.

2.   As newborn babes, desire the sincere milk of the word, that ye may grow thereby.— I Peter 2:2.

3.   What? know ye not that your body is the temple of the Holy Ghost which is in you, which ye have of God, and ye are not your own?
    For ye are bought with a price: therefore glorify God in your body, and in your spirit, which are God's.— I Corinthians 6:19, 20.

4.   Jesus saith unto him, I am the way, the truth, and the life: no man cometh unto the Father, but by me.— John 14:6.

5.   I have set watchmen upon thy walls, O Jerusalem, which shall never hold their peace day nor night: ye that make mention of the Lord, keep not silence,

And give him no rest, till he establish, and till he make Jerusalem a praise in the earth.— Isaiah 62:6, 7.

6.   And he spake a parable unto them to this end, that men ought always to pray, and not to faint.— Luke 18:1.

7.   Praying always with all prayer and supplication in the Spirit, and watching thereunto with all perseverance and supplication for all saints.— Ephesians 6:18.

Other Christians are always talking about "witnessing." I wince when I think about barging into somebody's life, preaching to him, and probably embarrassing us both. Furthermore, I don't like the ostentatious, show-off kind of Christian who hides his not-so-subtle bragging under a thin cloak of testimony. Maybe I could just keep quiet about it . . . I wonder . . . do I have to speak out for Christ?

7

DO I HAVE TO TESTIFY?

First reaction to this question is: "How can you help it?" True testimony or witnessing consists of vastly more than the spoken word. If you're real, you'll be bound to say something for Christ.

Please bear carefully in mind: Whether you are in the will of God or not, whether saved or unsaved, you are most emphatically giving a witness all the time — a witness to *whatever rules your life*. Like it or not, some of us are witnessing to our selfishness, our laziness, our lusts, our sub rosa love of the world, our shallowness, vanity and pride — oh, a thousand other things!

You never successfully conceal anything. You are witness to whatever you *are* down deep in your heart. "For out of the abundance of the heart the mouth speaketh."[1]

The increasing tendency to leave all effective

witnessing to the clergy, or to the eager-beaver type of Christian layfolk, is based not upon a valid distinction between talents, but upon sheer laziness or lack of true Christian experience.

Notice the significance of Acts 1:8 in this connection. The disciples had so far been witnesses only to their own cowardice and fear; to their low viewpoint of the Kingdom as a restore-Israel type of program; and to their utterly insular point of view, so far as help for the world was concerned. Now the Lord Jesus tells them, "There is going to be a new power that rules your lives. You will be controlled by the Holy Spirit. He will constrain you to speak of Me . . . not only where you are now, but reaching out into Judea and Samaria, then unto the uttermost part of the world."

Successful witnessing never was a matter of determination on the part of the early church. They never did urge each other to testify. It was not a matter of conscience even. They simply reacted normally to the lordship of the Holy Spirit. They were genuine. Even in their failure before and immediately after Calvary, they were utterly unposed. Similarly, when the blessed Spirit of God came upon them and began to speak through them, it was not a matter of trying but of glad surrender to His presence and power.

We border on the rankest hypocrisy when we *try* to do anything that takes a miracle to be genuine.

Use your will where it belongs — in willing to do God's will; in determining by God's grace to pray every day and read the Word of God regularly, and in willing to turn away from every appearance of evil.

Rely on *His will* and *His Spirit* when it comes to the matter of a relationship so important that it involves the salvation of a precious soul. Why, do you think, did the Lord Jesus emphasize so often the fact that the Holy Spirit would be given to guide, to bring to remembrance His words, to put proper words into disciples' trembling lips, to teach them what to say? Was it not that the Lord Jesus knows the awful impotence of the human brain, the perversity of the human tongue, and the utter impossibility of changing lives by mere talk!

A posed witness is a falsehood. The best witness is spontaneous. What you are will lead to what you say. If what you are is low-grade, sinful, worldly, carnal, self-centered, then *you are now witnessing to that fact*, and soiling with guilty fingers all the lives you touch!

Get in touch with the Lord Jesus Christ.

By prayer — real prayer that breaks your heart and moistens your eyes.

By eating the Word (Jer. 15:16), a process that takes some time every day.

By consciously cultivating the love of your Saviour, and casting out everything that you know grieves Him.

By consciously surrendering to the Holy Spirit (Eph. 5:18; Rom. 12:1).

God does not want your talents — not even the gift of gab!

He wants you, in a brokenhearted, sincere, now-and-forever kind of surrender that will make an effective Christian witness out of *everything* you say or do.

Having said all this, here are some pointers for successful witnessing:

1. Get over the mental hurdle involved in "talking religion" to people. Actually you talk to folk about every conceivable subject from morning to night. The only trouble about speaking for Christ is that you are unfamiliar with the subject, and so do not speak without restraint, but rather with some degree of embarrassment. Resolve to be willing to speak naturally of the greatest subject in the world, the Lord Jesus Christ, whenever you have op-

portunity to choose your own subject of conversation. (On this matter, see *Taking Men Alive* by Trumbull.)

2. Fill your mind and heart with the Word of God. "I will speak of thy testimonies . . . and will not be ashamed."[2] You speak naturally and unposedly only about material that has gotten down into your subconscious, or below-routine level of thinking. Hide God's Word in your heart and you will find yourself speaking of it, living by it, illustrating its truth by your character and conduct, and in general, having a highly effective witness as a result.

Question: How long has it been since you mastered a Scripture verse? Try one today, and say it over at intervals all day long; then review it once a day for seven weeks. At the end of that time you will have the scripture, but — more important — it will also have you! (Write to the Navigators, Colorado Springs, Colorado, for material on hiding God's Word in your heart.)

3. Begin each day with prayer for God's guidance and form the habit of watching throughout the day for the people God will send to you for your ministry to them. He knows whom you can help, and He can put you in touch with them.

4. Always rely on the Holy Spirit to tell you

what to say. Pray before you begin conversations, or even a telephone chat with some unknown caller. The Holy Spirit will lead you to use a scripture, a telling thought that, quite unknown to you, will be the final link in the chain of events that leads to someone's salvation.

Never depend upon smart logic, or smooth conversation to do the work either of conviction or conversion. Only the Holy Spirit using the Word can do that. Let Him.[3]

5. Always press gently for some action NOW. It may be only a word of prayer where you are talking together . . . or it may be you will have the joy of leading your friend directly to Jesus.

A demonstration (Rom. 12:2b) without a sale (Acts 2:37) is worth very little. We are to prove what is good and acceptable and perfect, namely, the will of God in Christ (John 6:40). A "sale" for the Christian soul-winner is that point at which your prospect is genuinely convicted by the Holy Spirit, senses his need, and asks for help. Get *some* action toward that desired result always before you leave.

6. Follow through. One contact may mean attention; another appreciation; but a third often means decision.

7. Soul-winning is a miracle. To try it in the energy of the flesh is fraudulent and sinful. God must do it through you, and He will, on the basis of Colossians 2:6 and Philippians 2:13. You received Christ by faith, now let Him operate through you by faith. When Jesus wins a soul, the work is well done! (See John 17:6-12.)

COORDINATE SCRIPTURE FOR CHAPTER 7

1. O generation of vipers, how can ye, being evil, speak good things? for out of the abundance of the heart the mouth speaketh. — Matthew 12:34.

2. I will speak of thy testimonies also before kings, and will not be ashamed. — Psalm 119:46.

3. So then faith cometh by hearing, and hearing by the word of God. — Romans 10:17.

Nevertheless I tell you the truth; It is expedient for you that I go away: for if I go not away, the Comforter will not come unto you; but if I depart, I will send him unto you.

And when he is come, he will reprove the world of sin, and of righteousness, and of judgment.—John 16:7, 8.

If I am fully surrendered will I have to become a preacher or a missionary? How will I know to what field God is calling me? How can I know I am in the will of God?

8

WHAT SHALL I DO WITH MY LIFE?

First of all, surrender it absolutely to God without qualification or reservation (Rom. 12:1).[1]

The best way to wreck your life and break your heart is by an incomplete surrender (compare Acts 5:1-11).[2]

The secret of unanswered prayer is incomplete surrender (Jas. 4:3).[3]

The question we must ask is not, "*How* will God use me?" but "Am I usable?"

Don't expect particular guidance without general surrender.

Do you know *how* to *surrender* to God? The secret is found in Luke 14:33: "Whosoever he be of you that forsaketh [renounceth] not all that he hath, he cannot be my disciple." That word *renounce* means to give up all claim to a thing or person. The way to surrender to God is to hand all that you have and are over to Him—renounce it.

Get a number of slips of paper. Write on one the amount of money you possess. On another your car. On another your family. On another your house. Continue until you have made a complete list of your dear ones and possessions. Last of all, write on one slip of paper the word, "Myself."

Now you are ready. Take those slips of paper one at a time and—if you really mean business with God—hand them over to Him. "Here, Lord, is my home, my car, my money, my dear ones, myself!"

Oh, to surrender to God! The surrendered life is the life God can use.

Start to live the kind of life God can bless, where you are. Don't wait until next month or next year for the opportunity that may make you great. God will only use the clean, yielded vessel (II Tim. 2:21).[4] Start being that kind of a vessel now.

Read up, and pray about, the needs of the world. You will be amazed at how little you know about the great missionary harvest fields of the world. Take a day to read about Africa and to pray for it. Another for India, and another for China. Still another for South America, and so on. By informing your mind, and intelligently obeying Luke 10:2, you give the Holy Spirit something to work on. Remember: Jesus never asked you to pray for a call. He *did* say: "Pray ye therefore the Lord of the harvest, that he would send forth laborers into his harvest." Start there, and let the rest be up to God.

Make a list of your talents and possibilities, and pray over them, asking God to reveal to you what field of endeavor you are best fitted for. Nothing is worse than a misfit, stumbling along trying to make a go of Christian service for which he is obviously not prepared. Similarly, there is nothing more bitter than the cry of a person who realizes too late that he should have been in the ministry or on the mission field, but got sidetracked into business or homemaking instead.

Get to work for God NOW. Start in your home, dealing with unsaved loved ones; consider your school or office or shop a place where you can serve and glorify God. In your church, be faithful in attendance and in keeping commitments (God will never use a slacker); be loyal to your pastor, and enthusiastic in inviting others to church. You may not be able to preach . . . but you can give out tracts and invitations to the services. When souls are won in this way, you will surely share in the reward at the judgment seat of Christ.

Consider the possibility of Bible school or a Bible-centered college, no matter what field you plan to enter. Mechanic or maestro, banker or bookworm, preacher or painter, you'll do better in your work after having spent two or more years with THE BOOK. "The fear of the Lord is the beginning of wisdom."

Do *right*. There is always a right thing to do. You may have many excuses and rationalizations for getting your own way, but when you meet the piercing eyes of the Lord Jesus, you will wish you had done the right thing. DO RIGHT. God will bless you and use you in it. "Thou meetest him that rejoiceth and worketh righteousness, those that remember thee in thy ways" (Isa. 64:5).

Above all, depend on God for every step. "Trust in the Lord with all thine heart; and lean not unto thine own understanding. In all thy ways acknowledge him and he shall direct thy paths" (Prov. 3:5, 6). God can make every hour, every day, a success. And what is a successful life but a series of successful days? Let the Holy Spirit guide. There are no regrets when He is in control.

ADMONITIONS

Always remember that your one business as a Christian is to aid in completing the evangelization of the world. "Into all the world . . . the gospel to every creature" is still the command of the Captain of our salvation. Your mind and heart will never go stale, your usefulness will constantly enlarge, if you keep a missionary vision bright and clear.

Never tolerate sin in your life. No day should go by without your being "prayed and confessed up to date." You may never see the morning light! A little sin leads to more sin, and before you know it, your joy is clouded, your testimony is ruined, and the Holy Spirit is grieved. Keep under the blood of Jesus . . . walk in the light, and fulfill I John 1:7.

It is dangerous to trifle with God. Remember Ananias and Sapphira (Acts 5). Remember Gehazi (II Kings 5:20-27). Remember King Saul (I Sam. 15:23). Remember Lot's wife (Gen. 19:26). You may pay *with your life* for refusing to judge your sins (I Cor. 11:28-32)!

Always follow through in obeying what God

told you when your knees were bent and your eyes were wet with tears. Never yield to cold-hearted rationalization that attempts to get your own way at the expense of God's will. You *may convince yourself*, but you'll still be wrong if you forsake the counsel He gave you in the sanctuary of your soul. Keep a tender conscience, and dare to obey what God tells you in the time of prayer. Remember: There are no regrets when He leads!

COORDINATE SCRIPTURE FOR CHAPTER 8

1.   I beseech you therefore, brethren, by the mercies of God, that ye present your bodies a living sacrifice, holy, acceptable unto God, which is your reasonable service. — Rom. 12:1.

2.   But a certain man named Ananias, with Sapphira his wife, sold a possession,

And kept back *part* of the price, his wife also being privy *to it*, and brought a certain part, and laid *it* at the apostles' feet.

But Peter said, Ananias, why hath Satan filled thine heart to lie to the Holy Ghost, and to keep back *part* of the price of the land?

Whiles it remained, was it not thine own? and

after it was sold, was it not in thine own power? Why hast thou conceived this thing in thine heart? thou hast not lied unto men, but unto God.

And Ananias, hearing these words, fell down, and gave up the ghost: and great fear came on all them that heard these things.

And the young men arose, wound him up, and carried *him* out, and buried *him*.

And it was about the space of three hours after, when his wife, not knowing what was done, came in.

And Peter answered unto her, Tell me whether ye sold the land for so much? And she said, Yea, for so much.

Then Peter said unto her, How is it that ye have agreed together to tempt the Spirit of the Lord? behold, the feet of them which have buried thy husband *are* at the door, and shall carry thee out.

Then fell she down straightway at his feet, and yielded up the ghost; and the young men came in, and found her dead, and, carrying *her* forth, buried *her* by her husband.

And great fear came upon all the church, and upon as many as heard these things. — Acts 5:1-11.

3. Ye ask, and receive not, because ye ask amiss, that ye may consume it upon your lusts. — James 4:3

4. If a man therefore purge himself from these, he

shall be a vessel unto honor, sanctified, and meet for the master's use, and prepared unto every good work. — II Tim. 2:21.

Now that I believe, where shall I draw the line in daily conduct? How can I know what is right and wrong? Can I take without question the ethics of my elders and other Christian friends? On the other hand, dare I disregard old-line standards? After all, who is to say whether I am holy or worldly — what makes the difference?

9

WORLDLINESS–AND WHAT TO DO ABOUT IT

You may as well face the facts: If you're born again, you are a different person. "Therefore, if any man be in Christ, he is a new creature."[1]

You have a new nature — the heavenly nature, begotten of God in you by the Holy Spirit. "But ye are not in the flesh, but in the Spirit, if so be that the Spirit of God dwell in you. Now if any man have not the Spirit of Christ, he is none of his" (Rom. 8:9).

You have a new citizenship — in a heavenly country: "For our conversation [citizenship, R.V.] is in heaven; from whence also we look for the Saviour, the Lord Jesus Christ" (Phil. 3:20).

You are moving toward a new destiny: "Who shall change our vile body, that it may be fashioned like unto his glorious body, according to the working whereby he is able even to subdue all things unto himself" (Phil. 3:21).

You are a pilgrim, not a resident: "Dearly beloved, I beseech you as strangers and pilgrims, abstain from fleshly lusts, which war against the soul" (I Pet. 2:11).

You have enlisted under a new Captain[2] and are engaged in a new kind of warfare.[3]

You have a new obligation — not to live after the flesh (old nature), but for God's glory.[4]

You have a new status — dead indeed unto sin, but alive unto God.[5]

You belong to a new family, and have new relatives: "But as many as received him, to them gave he power to become the sons of God even to them that believe on his name. . . . Now therefore ye are no more strangers and foreigners, but fellow citizens with the saints, and of the household of God" (Eph. 2:19).

You have a new occupation — to glorify God. "For ye are bought with a price; therefore glorify God in your body, and in your spirit, which are God's . . . (I Cor. 6:20). Whether therefore ye eat, or drink, or whatsoever ye do, do all to the glory of God . . . (I Cor. 10:31). And whatsoever ye do, do it heartily, as to the Lord, and not unto men . . . (Col. 3:23). Created in

114

Christ Jesus unto good works, which God hath before ordained that we should walk in them . . .[6] I will that thou affirm constantly that they which have believed in God might be careful to maintain good works."[7]

You will never be the same again — *never.* Try to explain it, rationalize it as you will, a Christian is different from unsaved people because he has been born again. God says so, and it is so.

If your Christianity is just a profession that can fit elastically over all forms of compromise, friend — you're lost! Get down on your knees and ask God to save you for Jesus' sake!

Another thing you may as well face is this: The world knows you are different since you've been born again.

Paul said, you remember, "Lord, they know that I imprisoned and beat in every synagogue them that believed on thee; and when the blood of thy martyr Stephen was shed, I also was standing by and consenting unto his death."[8]

Yes, they know. They know what you were, and what you are. They watch your every move to see whether you are real, or a sham. They listen to see whether your speech betrays the accent of Heaven, or the old words and phrases. They know — and they expect you to measure up.

When you compromise and play with the world, the most surprised person of all is the worldling. He may not have understood you ("Wherein they think it strange that ye run not with them to the same excess of riot, speaking evil of you" [I Pet. 4:41]), and he may have hated you ("Because ye are not of the world, but I have chosen you out of the world, therefore the world hateth you"[9]), but he will be surprised and disappointed when you lower Christ's blood-stained banner into the dust, and stoop to become a spiritual quisling when you could have been a conqueror!

Think through, now, in your own heart and mind, these facts:

* If I'm born again, I'm different, and will never be the same.

* The world knows I'm different, expects me to be different, and will be surprised and critical if I'm not.

This is the meaning of Romans 6:11 — "Likewise reckon ye also yourselves to be dead indeed unto sin, but alive unto God through Jesus Christ our Lord" (Rom. 6:11). Reckon . . . think . . . count on it . . . turn it over

in your mind until you REALLY believe it . . .
reckon yourself dead to sin.

Believe me: Until you have done this thing
— reckoning — thinking through — the fact
that you are dead to the world and alive to God
. . . until you have made up your mind to that
fact, you will always be irked by high Christian standards, and you'll never be completely,
spontaneously happy in God's will. A dead
man is the most completely *un*-bothered person you could imagine; and a resurrected person has the most overflowing joy of anyone
around him. That's it: Dead . . . to sin. Alive
(resurrected) . . . to God.

Discover now for yourself the basic process
of human life. Living . . . is surrendering . . . to
someone.

All your life before you were saved, you
surrendered to self and sin. "Trespasses and
sins, wherein in time past ye walked according
to the course of this world, according to the
prince of the power of the air, the spirit that
now worketh in the children of disobedience."[10]

Now your condition is changed. You are a
child of God, a subject of Heaven. You have
the privilege of surrendering, not to sin but to
your new Sovereign, and your new Friend —

the Lord Jesus Christ. "Neither yield ye your members as instruments of righteousness unto sin: but yield yourselves unto God, as those that are alive from the dead, and your members as instruments of righteousness unto God."[11]

If I am truly to surrender to the Lord Jesus Christ, then the simplest way to determine right conduct will be to relate *everything* to Him.

Concerning anything questionable, ask the following:

● Will this thing honor Him, please Him, or grieve Him?

● Will it obey Him, or disobey Him?

● Is it in line with what I KNOW to be His will?

● Does it build up the kind of character and spiritual life that glorifies Him?

● Does it identify me with His followers, or with the world's crowd?

● Will it stand the test of His eyes and holiness at the judgment seat of Christ?

● Does this thing help, or hinder my prayer life?

● Does this thing help or hinder my reading and study and assimilation of His Word?

Remember: "And whatsoever ye do in word

or deed, do all in the name of the Lord Jesus, giving thanks to God and the Father by him."[12]

Secondarily, your relationship with your Christian brothers and sisters is involved. Paul said: "Wherefore, if meat make my brother to offend, I will eat no flesh while the world standeth, lest I make my brother to offend . . . when ye sin so against the brethren, and wound their weak conscience, ye sin against Christ."[13] "Judge this," said the apostle, "that no man put a stumbling block or an occasion to fall in his brother's way."[14]

People *do* watch you, you know. What you may not realize is that *there are individuals right now who are patterning their conduct after yours.* Somebody, somewhere, is a carbon copy of you. What if he is reproducing your selfishness, your weakness, your compromise, your sin? Oh, flee now to the fountain filled with blood, and let Jesus cleanse the heart, renew the life, so that it may be the kind of example He wants it to be. "Let all things," pleads Paul, "be done unto edifying [building up]" (I Cor. 14:26b).

The question now is not "How much may I indulge in, and still be saved?" God forbid! I must rather ask, "What about Christ's will, and what about the example I set for my fellow Christians?

This is not all, however. Your relationship to the world of the unsaved, and to the demons, even to Satan himself, is involved.

Consider Satan. Is he interested in tearing down your testimony? Read Job 1 and 2 for your answer. Satan would like to lead you into sin so he could go back and laugh in the face of God and taunt Him about you! Are you going to give him that chance?

Consider the enemies of God. Read II Samuel 12:9-14. "By this deed," says Nathan, "thou hast given great occasion to the enemies of the Lord to blaspheme!" Are you going to go weakly into compromise and sin, and give God-hating people all around you an opportunity to blaspheme and curse God, grieving His heart afresh, and reopening the wounds of Calvary? Think before you act.

You don't need any list of "dos" and "don'ts" as a Christian. All you need to keep straight is the thorough knowledge that you're born again . . . a real surrender to Christ . . . a loving concern for your fellows . . . a genuine hatred for Satan and sin . . . and a healthy fear of God. The rest is up to Him, for "He which hath begun a good work in you will perform it until the day of Jesus Christ,"[15] and "it is God which worketh in you both to will and to do of his good pleasure" (Phil. 2:13).

COORDINATE SCRIPTURE FOR CHAPTER 9

1.   Therefore if any man be in Christ, he is a new creature: old things are passed away; behold, all things are become new. — II Corinthians 5:17.

2.   For it became him, for whom are all things, and by whom are all things, in bringing many sons unto glory, to make the captain of their salvation perfect through sufferings. — Hebrews 2:10.

3.   Thou therefore endure hardness, as a good soldier of Jesus Christ. — II Timothy 2:3.

Wherefore take unto you the whole armor of God, that ye may be able to withstand in the evil day, and having done all, to stand.

Stand therefore, having your loins girt about with truth, and having on the breastplate of righteousness;

And your feet shod with the preparation of the gospel of peace;

Above all, taking the shield of faith, wherewith ye shall be able to quench all the fiery darts of the wicked.

And take the helmet of salvation, and the sword of the Spirit, which is the word of God:

Praying always with all prayer and supplication in the Spirit, and watching thereunto with all perseverance and supplication for all saints.
—Ephesians 6:13-18.

4.   Therefore brethren, we are debtors, not to the flesh, to live after the flesh.

For if ye live after the flesh, ye shall die: but if ye through the Spirit do mortify the deeds of the body, ye shall live.—Romans 8:12, 13.

5.   Likewise reckon ye also yourselves to be dead indeed unto sin, but alive unto God through Jesus Christ our Lord.—Romans 6:11.

6.   For we are his workmanship, created in Christ Jesus unto good works, which God hath before ordained that we should walk in them.
—Ephesians 2:10.

7.   This is a faithful saying, and these things I will that thou affirm constantly, that they which have believed in God might be careful to maintain good works. These things are good and profitable unto men.—Titus 3:8.

8.   And I said, Lord, they know that I imprisoned and beat in every synagogue them that believed on thee:

And when the blood of thy martyr Stephen was

shed, I also was standing by, and consenting unto his death, and kept the raiment of them that slew him. — Acts 22:19, 20.

9. If ye were of the world, the world would love his own: but because ye are not of the world, but I have chosen you out of the world, therefore the world hateth you. — John 15:19.

10. And you hath he quickened, who were dead in trespasses and sins:

Wherein in time past ye walked according to the course of this world, according to the prince of the power of the air, the spirit that now worketh in the children of disobedience. — Ephesians 2:1, 2.

11. Neither yield ye your members as instruments of unrighteousness unto sin: but yield yourselves unto God, as those that are alive from the dead, and your members as instruments of righteousness unto God.

For sin shall not have dominion over you: for ye are not under the law, but under grace.

What then? shall we sin, because we are not under the law, but under grace? God forbid.

Know ye not, that to whom ye yield yourselves servants to obey, his servants ye are to whom ye obey; whether of sin unto death, or of obedience unto righteousness?

But God be thanked, that ye were the servants of

sin, but ye have obeyed from the heart that form of doctrine which was delivered you.

Being then made free from sin, ye became the servants of righteousness.

I speak after the manner of men because of the infirmity of your flesh: for as ye have yielded your members servants to uncleanness and to iniquity unto iniquity; even so now yield your members unto holiness.

For when ye were the servants of sin, ye were free from righteousness.

What fruit had ye then in those things whereof ye are now ashamed? for the end of those things is death.

But now being made free from sin, and become servants to God, ye have your fruit unto holiness, and the end everlasting life.

For the wages of sin is death; but the gift of God is eternal life through Jesus Christ our Lord. —Romans 6:13-23.

12.   And whatsoever ye do in word or deed, do all in the name of the Lord Jesus, giving thanks to God and the Father by him.—Colossians 3:17.

13.   But when ye sin so against the brethren, and wound their weak conscience, ye sin against Christ.

Wherefore, if meat make my brother to offend, I will eat no flesh while the world standeth, lest I make my brother to offend. — I Corinthians 8:12, 13.

14. Let us not therefore judge one another any more: but judge this rather, than no man put a stumbling block or an occasion to fall in his brother's way. — Romans 14:13.

15. Being confident of this very thing, that he which hath begun a good work in you will perform it until the day of Jesus Christ. — Philippians 1:6.

Moody Press, a ministry of the Moody Bible Institute, is designed for education, evangelization and edification. If we may assist you in knowing more about Christ and the Christian life, please write us without obligation to: Moody Press, c/o MLM, Chicago, Illinois 60610.